THE ZEBRA

BY
CARL R. GREEN
WILLIAM R. SANFORD

EDITED BY
JUDY LOCKWOOD

PUBLISHED BY
CRESTWOOD HOUSE
Mankato, MN, U.S.A.

CIP

LIBRARY OF CONGRESS CATALOGING IN PUBLICATION DATA

Green, Carl R.
  The zebra

  (Wildlife, habits & habitat)
  Includes index.
  SUMMARY: Examines the physical characteristics, behavior, lifestyle and natural environment of the zebra.
  1. Zebras—Juvenile literature. [1. Zebras.] I. Sanford, William R. (William Reynolds), 1927-   II. Lockwood, Judy.   III. Title.   IV. Series.
QL737.U62G74   1988   599.72'5—dc19   88-1831
ISBN 0-89686-388-3

International Standard Book Number:	Library of Congress Catalog Card Number:
0-89686-388-3	88-1831

PHOTO CREDITS:

Cover: Tom Stack & Associates (Charles G. Summers, Jr.)
DRK Photo: (M.P. Kahl) 4, 7, 13, 24, 37; (Stephen J. Krasemann) 14, 21, 27, 30, 35; (Peter D. Pickford) 18, 33
Tom Stack & Associates: (Susan Gibler) 8, 41; (Charles G. Summers, Jr.) 10, 22; (Leonard Lee Rue III) 12; (Bill Tronca) 16; (F.S. Mitchell) 26

Produced by Carnival Enterprises.

CRESTWOOD HOUSE

Box 3427, Mankato, MN, U.S.A. 56002

TABLE OF CONTENTS

Scientists debate whether a zebra is black with white stripes or white with black stripes.

INTRODUCTION:

The great zebra debate started when Mrs. Wilhite wrote a new spelling word on the board. The students wrote the word in their notebooks: C-A-M-O-U-F-L-A-G-E.

"This word is easier to say than it is to spell," Mrs. Wilhite said. "Can anyone tell me what it means?"

Sid's hand shot up. "Soldiers wear camouflage so enemies can't see them," he said. "Good camouflage makes them invisible, so they won't get shot."

The teacher smiled. "You have got the right idea, Sid. Camouflage is a pattern of shapes and colors that makes something blend in with its background. It may not be invisible, but it will be hard to see."

Penny looked thoughtful. "My dad says that animals were using camouflage long before soldiers did," she said.

"That's right!" Fred broke in. "A lion's coat is the color of dry grass. That makes it easier for the lion to sneak up on its prey. A tiger's stripes are camouflage, too. The tiger blends in with the jungle's pattern of sun and shade." A puzzled look came over his face. "So, how do you explain the zebra's stripes? Zebras live out on the open plains. It looks to me as if their stripes would make them easier to see, not harder."

"That's a good question, Fred," Mrs. Wilhite

replied. "The naturalists are still working on that one."

Penny's hand was up again. "The earliest horses had stripes and spots much like zebras," she said. "I learned that when I did a report on horses last year. Modern horses lost their stripes a long time ago, but zebras kept theirs."

"That may be," Fred said quickly, "but it doesn't explain *why* the zebra has stripes!"

Mrs. Wilhite cut off the debate before it could go further. "Let's agree that a zebra's stripes aren't much good as camouflage," she said. "The zebra never 'freezes' when it senses danger. It runs away, and those moving stripes must be easy to see. Also, with only a few trees around, a herd of zebras can't hide in the shadows. Can you think of any good use for black-and-white stripes?"

Mary remembered something her mother had told her. "Maybe it's for heat control," she said. "The white areas reflect the sun and keep the animal cooler. It does get hot in Africa."

Mrs. Wilhite nodded. "That's a good theory," she agreed. "According to another theory, the stripes confuse attacking predators. When the herd starts to run, the stripes all become one big blur. Just for an instant, a lion might not be able to tell one zebra from another. That moment of confusion might give the zebras time to escape."

"Another theory is that some insects are confused

A zebra herd is easily startled.

by the narrow stripes. They fly past the zebras and bite other animals. One last theory relates the stripes to a zebra's social life. Every zebra's stripes are different, just like your fingerprints. Maybe the stripes help the animals recognize each other. Or, think of it this way—stripes mean friends, no stripes mean possible danger. One study showed that zebras are attracted to stripes; they shy away from solid colors."

"Which theory is true?" Penny wanted to know.

"No one knows," Mrs. Wilhite said. "Maybe more

than one is true. For now, I want all of you to do some reading on these interesting animals. Maybe you'll find the answer to another question: are zebras white animals with black stripes, or black animals with white stripes?"

A stallion, mares, and their foals make up a zebra family.

CHAPTER ONE

The zebra is a living riddle. Are those black stripes on a white animal? Or is it a black animal with white stripes?

The experts don't have a final answer. Some naturalists point out that the skin on the zebra's belly and inside its legs is white. Therefore, they say, the zebra is white with black stripes. Other scientists shake their heads in disagreement. They point out that a few zebras are almost black when they are born. Their "stripes" are only rows of white dots and dashes. These scientists argue that when nature goes back to the original color, that color is black.

Who's right? The zebras aren't telling.

A family known as the Equids

White or black, zebras are mammals. They belong to a family of hoofed, plant-eating animals called the *perissodactyla*. Other members of the family are the rhinoceros and the tapir. The perissodactyls all have an odd number of toes. The zebra branch of the family is known as the *equidae*. The horse and the wild ass (donkey) are the zebra's close cousins.

Burchell's zebra is a short-legged, fat-looking animal.

Eohippus (the zebra's earliest ancestor) developed in North America over three million years ago. It had toes and was no bigger than a fox. As eohippus became larger, its toes grew together to form a solid hoof. Now known as *equus,* the early horse wandered north and crossed a land bridge that connected Alaska and Asia. Later, when the glaciers melted, the bridge vanished under the waters of the Bering Strait. About eight thousand years ago, equus became extinct in the Americas. Naturalists guess that Native American hunters killed them for food.

Three species of zebra

Only three species of zebra are still alive today. All live in Africa. The zebras most often seen in films and at the zoo are forms of the plains zebra, also known as Burchell's zebra.

All plains zebras tend to be short-legged, fat-looking animals. They differ mostly in their markings. Chapman's zebra has stripes that stop a little below the knee. Light grey "shadow stripes" show between the black stripes. Grant's zebra *boehmi,* by contrast, has stripes almost to the hoofs. Most zebras have a short, bristly mane, but Grant's zebra often has none at all. Finally, Selous' zebra wears stripes down to the hoofs and rarely shows shadow stripes.

Mountain zebras are smaller animals with reddish-brown stripes.

The mountain zebra lives to the south and southwest of the plains zebra. Mountain zebras are small, stocky animals with broad stripes that stop short of their bellies. The stripes on the face are reddish-brown in color. Mountain zebras have a dewlap, which is an extra flap of skin just under their jaw.

The largest of all zebras is Grévy's zebra. With its long, narrow head, this species looks a little like a mule, (a cross between a horse and a donkey). It has

Grévy's zebra has a long, narrow head and resembles a mule.

large, rounded ears and many narrow stripes. The belly is unstriped, but the legs are striped down to the hoofs. Grévy's zebras range from southern Ethiopia to northern Kenya.

A pony-sized animal

A zebra is about three-fourths the size of a wild horse. An average stallion (a mature male) weighs

A pregnant mare will carry her foal for 11 to 13 months.

about 770 pounds (350 kilograms). From nose to rump, it measures from 80 to 96 inches (203 to 244 centimeters) long. At the shoulder, a zebra measures 50 to 64 inches (127 to 163 cm) tall. The stallions average ten percent larger than the mares (the mature females).

A zebra's tail adds about two feet (0.6 m) to the animal's length. Unlike that of the horse, a zebra's tail is not all hair. The upper part is solid cartilage, ending in long black and white hairs. The zebra uses its tail as a fly whisk, but it can also signal anger. Several violent tail switches tell other zebras to stay away.

A life on the hoof

A zebra's body is designed for two purposes: eating grass and escaping from predators. A zebra's body builds up layers of fat that is stored for times of drought when grass is hard to find. To outrun the lions who prey upon it, the zebra needs speed, agility, and endurance. Its strong heart, big lungs, and long legs give it these abilities.

Naturalists tell us that a zebra runs on the tip of its third toe! As equus was developing, the third toe became larger, and the other toes were lost. The hard, horn-like hoof is really an overgrown toenail. The shape of the hoof depends on where the zebra lives. Plains zebras have hoofs with broad, rounded lower rims. Mountain zebras have high, narrow hoofs. This shape gives them better footing on rocky trails.

For short bursts of speed, a zebra has been clocked at 60 miles (96 km) per hour. On a longer run, it can average 30 to 40 miles (48 to 64 km) per hour. Extremely agile, the zebra can turn sharply to either side. Even when a herd is running at top speed, the animals never seem to trip over one another.

People who ride horses would recognize the zebra's basic gaits (the ways it walks or runs). The walk is a four-beat movement — left front, right rear, right front, left rear. When the zebra trots, it changes to a

A zebra's mane is made of stiff black-and-white hair.

16

two-beat gait. Left front and right rear legs move together, then right front and left rear. A frightened zebra moves into a gallop by springing forward off its powerful rear legs. All four hoofs leave the ground during the gallop.

Teeth, neck, and mane

When feeding, the zebra's strong lips pull the grass into its mouth. Twelve curved, chisel-like incisors (cutting teeth) chop the grass off close to the ground. The tongue moves the food back to the 24 molars and premolars. There are six of these grinding teeth on each side of the upper and lower jaws. The zebra's teeth continue to grow throughout its lifetime. Otherwise, its diet of tough, gritty grass would wear down the teeth. A toothless zebra would soon starve. Stallions also have four canines (ripping teeth) to use for fighting.

With its long neck, the zebra bends low to graze and rises up high to watch for danger. The zebra can also swing its flexible neck sideways to nibble at insect bites. Its hide is covered with a coat of short, black-and-white hair. A mane of stiff hair grows on the back of its neck. All zebras are born with manes, but Grant's zebra sheds its mane when it matures.

Zebras are always alert and ready to run away from danger.

Zebras depend on their eyes

The zebra's keen, bulging eyes are set high on its skull. The wide angle lenses of its eyes allow the zebra to see to the side and rear. The only place a zebra can't see is behind its own rump. Any movement behind a zebra causes it to shy away until the zebra identifies the movement. Besides good daytime vision, the zebra can see very well at night.

Zebras also depend on their noses and ears. A grazing zebra pauses, raises its head, and flares its large nostrils. It tests the wind for signs of a lurking predator. At the same time, the animal moves its ears forward and backward like radar disks. Any unusual sound, no matter how slight, puts the zebra on guard. When the ears are pointing forward, the zebra is signaling fear. Pulled back, the ears signal anger.

The zebra needs all of its senses if it is to survive. Its African habitat is rich not only in food and water, but also in predators.

CHAPTER TWO

The best places to see zebras are on the open, rolling grasslands known as savannahs. Plains zebras range along Africa's east coast savannahs, from the tip of the Persian Gulf almost to the Cape of Good Hope. Mountain zebras live in hilly country, inland from the west coast.

Some zebra stallions live alone, but that's unusual for this social animal. A single herd of zebras may number 10,000 animals! On Tanzania's Serengeti Plain, smaller herds sometimes join to create superherds of 150,000 animals. When that happens, zebras cover the savannah almost as far as the eye can see.

Life in a zebra herd

Most zebras belong to a family group within the herd. The family groups, often called harems, don't fight for territory. They are always on the move, seeking the best grass to eat and water to drink. When conflicts arise, it's because a stallion is trying to steal a mare from another stallion's harem.

A typical harem consists of a stallion, his mares, and that year's foals (newborn zebras). A few stallions

A zebra herd may contain 10,000 animals.

keep as many as six mares, but most have only two or three. Each stallion rules his own harem, but the mares maintain a lively independence. The oldest mare, for example, leads the harem from place to place. Each mare has her place in the line of march. If a mare tries to move up, the others bite and kick her until she returns to her old place.

The mares within a harem keep to themselves, but the stallions are more social. They seek out and "greet" stallions from other groups. The stallions whinny, extend their necks, and sniff noses. Then they rear up in a farewell gesture before returning to their mares. The stallions repeat this greeting with each new family they meet.

A harem stallion travels behind his mares and foals. From this position, he can defend the harem and keep his wandering foals in line. If a mare or foal becomes separated from the harem, the others stop and search for it. A stallion will look for any mare or foal, but mares search only for their own foals.

The oldest mare leads her family from place to place while the stallion guards the back.

Fillies and colts leave the harem

When a female foal is 18 to 24 months of age, she becomes a filly. Now that she is ready to mate, other stallions gallop in and try to steal her. Surrounded by eager opponents, the harem stallion soon loses this battle. The successful theft usually comes when he is chasing away one of the other stallions. Once captured as fillies, the mares become loyal. They prefer to stay with the stallion that steals them from the harem where they were born. In the new harem, the older mares use their teeth and hoofs to keep the newcomer in her place. It takes about six months for her to be fully accepted into the group.

A one-year-old male foal is called a colt. Colts leave the harem sometime between their first and fourth birthdays. At first, the colts join a bachelor herd made up of 3 to 15 other colts. Led by an older stallion, the bachelors seem to have a good time running, fighting, and playing. Most colts remain bachelors until they're five- or six-year-old stallions. Then they try to form their own harems. Since each harem stallion controls several mares, there are always bachelors left over.

An adult zebra can eat 20 pounds of grass a day!

A life spent grazing

Most of a zebra's waking hours are spent grazing. Soon after sunrise, the herd walks single file to the grasslands. Zebras feed side-by-side with wildebeests, impalas, and other grazing animals. Each species feeds on different grasses, so there is food for all.

Zebras are the only grazing animals on the

savannahs that have both upper and lower incisors. This lets them bite off the top half of the grass stem instead of pulling it out by the roots. An adult zebra eats about 20 pounds (9 kg) of tough, coarse grasses a day. The bacteria in its digestive system help break down the fibers and free the food energy.

The herd makes its first trip to a water hole in mid-morning. Zebras know that lions may be nearby, so they approach with caution. When the leaders are sure it's safe, they lower their heads and drink. The animals may splash about in shallow water, but fear of crocodiles keeps them from going deeper. The herd also visits a salt lick once or twice a week. A salt lick is a natural deposit of rock salt in the earth. Like all wild animals, zebras need salt to keep their body fluids in balance.

Keeping clean takes time

When they're not eating, zebras take care of their coats, a process called grooming. The animals stand shoulder to shoulder, and each zebra nibbles at its partner's neck. This cleans hard-to-reach places. Grooming also builds friendships between zebras. Like happy children, they roll over and over in dust and mud wallows. A coating of dust or mud protects them from insects. The zebras rub against large rocks, tree trunks, and termite mounds to get rid of ticks and itchy dead skin. Tickbirds do a similar job. The birds perch on the zebra's back and eat the insects they find there.

Zebras rest during the early afternoon. As night falls, the herd moves into an open area where the stallions can easily spot predators. Foals lie down to sleep, but the older animals often sleep standing up. If they do lie down, they sleep on their sides. One or more stallions stand watch at all times.

A low branch makes a good scratching post for this zebra.

The lion's favorite meal

Zebras are a favorite prey animal for lions, wild dogs, hyenas, and leopards. Lions kill more zebras than any other predator. The sight of a lion chasing a herd of zebras makes it look as though the zebra is a coward. That isn't true. Zebras don't panic at the sight of a lion. They go on grazing, keeping a wary eye on the lion. The herd runs only when the lion is close

When a lion is ready to spring, the zebra herd runs away fast.

and ready to spring. Similarly, zebras show no fear of humans. If angered, they will charge. More than one careless hunter has been trampled to death by zebras.

Healthy, well-fed zebras have lived as long as 29 years. Disease and accident, however, probably kill more zebras than do predators. Flies and ticks are the most common insect pests. Most zebras also are infested with roundworms, tapeworms, and lung-worms. The animal is immune to sleeping sickness, a disease that affects horses and mules. But tetanus may develop in wounds left by a lion's claws. Falls sometimes result in broken legs. If the injured zebra can keep up with the herd, the other zebras will protect it. Given time for the leg to heal, the zebra is able to live normally.

CHAPTER THREE:

A noon sun blazes over Kenya's Nairobi National Park. The rains ended in January. Now, in late February, the long grass is turning dry and yellow. The sound of hoofbeats breaks the silence. A herd of plains zebras thunders across the savannah. Clouds of dust hang in the air behind them.

The herd's leaders come to a stop. The pack of wild dogs that stampeded them has given up the chase. The zebras bend down to sample the long grass. As they do so, a stallion named Kiji and his mare, Zia, catch up with the rest of the herd. The stallion had stayed behind to protect the slow-moving mare. It's almost time for Zia's foal to be born.

Birth of a foal

Zia is eight years old, and this will be her third foal. The first was born when she was only four. Both foals were fillies, and both have left the harem to mate with younger stallions. As with most zebra foals, the fillies were born between January and March. Mares carry their foals for 11 to 13 months.

As the herd grazes, Zia leaves the others and beds down in a grassy hollow. Kiji whinnies softly but doesn't follow. Instinct tells him to leave Zia alone. He keeps an eye out for predators, though. Hyenas and wild dogs can grab a newborn foal and be gone in an instant.

The birth goes quickly once it starts. Zia is standing when the foal's two front black hoofs and nose first appear. She lies down and the birth is soon over. The newcomer, Neo, is a male foal. Zia licks Neo's rough, brown and white coat to clean him. The brown will turn to black later on. Neo struggles to his feet five minutes after being born. He topples over, but he tries again. Finally, he stands upright, shaky on his long legs.

Zebra foals are born with brown-and-white hides.

Kiji gives a warning snort. Zia sniffs the breeze and picks up the scent of hyenas. The herd shifts restlessly, but Neo knows only that he's hungry. He finds one of Zia's two teats and begins to nurse. The foal looks tiny next to her, but he weighs almost 90 pounds (41 kg). When he's standing to nurse, he measures almost exactly three feet (0.9 m) at the shoulder.

An hour later, Neo trots after Zia when she rejoins the harem. The sun slides swiftly below the horizon. That's the signal for the herd to move to its nighttime resting place. The harem's oldest mare leads the small family group in single file. Kiji brings up the rear, still on guard.

Neo grows quickly

By the time the dry season reaches its peak in March, Neo has lost his baby fuzz. Black stripes show clearly on his sleek, well-fed body. After nursing, Neo plays tag and chase games with other foals. The games build up his speed and agility. Kiji playfully fights with Neo, teaching him to rear, kick, and bite. Those lessons will be important when Neo must fight for mates.

The herd travels long distances to find grass and water. Every trip is an adventure for Neo. He learns to recognize danger signals of the herd and of the other animals. The cawing of a crow and the sudden stampede of the gazelle tell him predators are near. Zia mated with Kiji soon after Neo's birth, and she is pregnant again. It's unusual for a mare to give birth two years in a row.

One of the harem's fillies, Alba, is two years old. Alba has been attracting other stallions. As long as they come in ones and twos, Kiji can drive them away. The short, sharp battles test the stallion's strength and speed. Only the strongest stallions can gain and keep harems. Kiji doesn't mate with his own fillies, but instinct tells him to keep them in the harem.

The wet season

The dry season ends in May with the coming of the long rains. The sudden downpour excites Neo. He dashes about, rain filling his eyes and streaming down his back. Within the week, fresh green grass is growing all across the savannah. The water holes and rivers fill with water. The herd huddles together under a stand of thorn trees to escape the pounding rain.

In this land below the equator, the winter months are reversed from what we know. June, July, and August are cool and wet. In September, the land warms up. The herd eats the tall grass hungrily. Neo is still nursing, but he's also learning to eat grass. Strong and frisky, Neo discovers the joy of teasing a rhinoceros. He races in circles around the slower animal. The powerful rhino shakes its head and stares at the running zebra.

The next day brings a different kind of adventure. The park rangers shoot Zia with a dart that puts her to sleep. Neo makes nervous little barking noises and nudges Zia's body. When the rangers come too close, he runs off to join Kiji. While Zia is asleep, the rangers measure her and take blood samples. The tests will let them know if the herd is healthy. An hour later, the

A foal can stand up and run a few minutes after birth.

mare scrambles to her feet. She nuzzles Neo to let him know she's all right.

A death in the family

By late October, Neo is a fully-weaned colt, 53 inches (135 cm) tall. The colts still play their running games, but there's more playful fighting now. They imitate the stallions, rearing and striking out with their hoofs. Sometimes they bang into each other for the sheer joy of physical contact. At night, the colts sometimes stand guard duty with the stallions.

As it often does with zebras, tragedy strikes suddenly. The herd is walking single file to a water hole one day. A lioness crouches silently in the overhanging trees. The big cat lets Kiji's harem pass by, then she drops onto his back. Her razor claws sink deeply into the stallion's neck. Neo, Zia, and the others stampede, leaving Kiji to fight for his life. Maddened with pain, the stallion tries to buck the lioness off. But it's no use. Moments later, he crashes to the ground. The timeless battle between predator and prey has taken another victim.

Kiji's harem waits for him a half mile away. When he doesn't join them, other stallions edge closer to the mares. Finally, a strong young stallion named Quag drives the others away. Quag herds Zia, Neo, and the others ahead of him. When they resist, he bites their necks. The harem has a new master.

The cycle is complete

The rains return in November and December. As Neo matures, Quag becomes jealous of him. The stallion will drive Neo out of the harem about the

During its life, a zebra faces many natural and manmade dangers.

time Zia gives birth in February. Neo will join a bachelor herd. In a few more years, he'll be ready to compete for his own harem.

The dangers of predators, disease, drought, and poachers lie ahead. If Neo survives, he'll mate and father a new generation of plains zebra foals.

CHAPTER FOUR:

Children learn about zebras at the same time they learn their ABC's. If *A* is for *Apple,* then *Z* must be for *Zebra.*

The name zebra probably comes from a Semitic word, *zibra.* Long ago, zibra referred to a guinea hen with black and white stripes. Since then, zebra has been used to describe almost anything that has black and white stripes. The list includes the zebra finch, the zebra fish, the zebra mouse, and the zebra butterfly. All, of course, wear black-and-white stripes.

Zebra shows up in other ways, too. Sports officials who wear striped shirts are sometimes called zebras! In England, people hurry across streets on painted black-and-white pathways called zebra crossings. You may hear people say, "A zebra can't change its stripes." That's a way of saying that someone is too set in his or her ways to change.

Taming and cross-breeding the zebra

Unlike some wild animals, zebras can be tamed. In the 1700s, a French naturalist reported that he had saddled and ridden a zebra. Later, zebras were used to replace horses and mules in East Africa. The domestic animals were dying from a form of sleeping sickness. Zebras are immune to the disease, so people captured them and used them as pack animals. In the 1820s, the London zoo used zebras to pull wagons through the streets of the city. Similarly, a milkman in St. Louis, Missouri, used zebras to pull his milk wagon in the 1920s.

People have tried to crossbreed zebras with other species of equus. In the wild, zebras never mate with another species. In captivity, mountain zebras have been crossbred with plains zebras, wild Somali asses, and domestic horses. When two different species

Zebras share their watering hole with other wild animals.

mate, the young produced are called hybrids. Zebra-horse hybrids are strong, easy to handle, and sure-footed. Like mules, the hybrids are sterile (unable to reproduce themselves).

Training or crossbreeding zebras hasn't produced a new domestic animal. Horses can do everything a zebra can do, and do it better. The zebra doesn't have the strength and endurance of the domestic horse. In the late 1800s, some farmers in Kenya tried raising zebras for meat and hides. Zebra farms, however, never made much money for the owners.

The zebra as a zoo animal

Zebras are popular zoo animals, but they're not easy to keep. Visitors like to feed them, but a hungry zebra will bite a finger as quickly as it will bite a carrot. Another problem is that a captive zebra's hoofs keep on growing. A keeper must trim the hoofs or the animal will go lame. The only way to do that is to put the zebra to sleep, and that's risky for the animal.

Some zoos have enough space to set up wild animal parks for their herd animals. Given enough room, zebras behave more naturally. Constant movement helps wear down their hoofs. The zoo's problems aren't over, however. Zebras have been known to kill impalas and other antelopes who share their range.

Lions aren't the only danger

Most African governments try to protect their wildlife. Sadly enough, however, there's money to be made from killing wild animals. Poachers sneak into game reserves to hunt rhinoceroses, hippos, zebras, and other animals. Sometimes a poacher takes only the zebra's tail and sells it to a tourist as a fly whisk. At other times, the hide is taken to make into a wall hanging. Modern poachers use off-road trucks and rifles to kill dozens of zebras in a few minutes. Natives who can't afford rifles use poisoned spears and arrows. They also set snares made of steel wire. A zebra caught in a snare dies a slow and painful death.

Naturalists say that loss of habitat is a greater danger than all the poachers put together. Africa needs food for people, and farmers who grow that food are moving into the zebra's habitat. Those acres not plowed up are often grazed by herds of goats, sheep, and cattle. The domestic animals eat the grass that once fed the zebra.

In the 1800s, an entire subspecies of zebra was wiped out by hunters. People who love wildlife use the story to remind everyone of what could happen to the remaining zebras.

CHAPTER FIVE:

The quagga (*equus quagga*) once lived on the South African plains in large numbers. In less than 100 years (from 1780 to 1880), the subspecies became extinct. How could an animal disappear so quickly? The story tells us a lot about human greed and carelessness.

A handsome member of the zebra family

The quagga was slightly taller and heavier than the plains zebra. Dark brown stripes ran from its head to its shoulders and then faded out. The rest of the body was a muddy chestnut brown. The quagga's mane stood erect and it had a flowing white tail. Observers thought the animal was the handsomest of all the zebras. They said that its coat actually sparkled!

The name "quagga" came from the barking noise the animal made, a sound like "qua-ha." Quaggas lived in what is now South Africa's Cape Province and the Orange Free State. Early settlers found that the species tamed easily. Some farmers used them as "watchdogs" to protect their cattle from hyenas.

Quaggas were easy game

The Dutch farmers who settled the region were called Boers. Killing quaggas, they said, provided meat for native servants. It also protected grasslands needed for grazing cattle and saved crops from being trampled.

The Boers took horse-drawn wagons out to the savannahs where the quaggas grazed. Each herd

To prevent their extinction, naturalists carefully study and protect zebras.

traveled in single file at a slow trot. When a rider cut across the front of a herd, the quaggas would stop and stare. Then they would start off in a new direction. This gave the hunters plenty of time to open fire. The hunters piled the dead quaggas into their wagons. If some of the bodies didn't fit, they left them to rot.

William John Burchell, an English naturalist, saw the quaggas in 1811-1812. He wrote that "the whole plain seemed alive and checkered black and white." Once the quaggas broke into a gallop, Burchell compared the sound to the noise of a cavalry charge. Riders who followed too closely were sometimes hit by rocks thrown up by the quaggas' hoofs. Wounded quaggas also were dangerous. One kick could crush a man's skull, and sharp teeth could bite off a hand.

The quagga is hunted to extinction

The Boers kept on with their quagga hunts. They tanned the hides and made them into baskets for harvesting their crops. The thicker leather from the quaggas' legs made good soles for homemade shoes. Later, it became the fashion to use a harness made from the striped section of a hide. By 1820, the quaggas were extinct in most of Cape Province. This was two-thirds of their range. As the Boers moved inland after 1850, the killing went on.

In 1858, a wildlife survey turned up only three wild quaggas. The last of these survivors was shot in 1861. After that, only the quaggas kept in zoos were left alive. The zookeepers didn't know that the animal was an endangered species. No extra effort was made to breed them. A few foals were born, but not enough. In 1883, the last surviving quagga died in an Amsterdam zoo. The zookeepers wired their African game suppliers to send more quaggas. The answer came back: "There aren't any more."

Naturalists still hope to find a lost herd of quaggas living in the mountains of Cape Province. Reports of quagga herds come in from time to time, but the animals always turn out to be mountain zebras. From a distance, seen through a heat haze, the two species look alike.

Grévy's zebra won't follow the quagga

William Gruenerwald doesn't want the big-eared Grévy's zebra to follow the quagga into extinction. To make sure it won't, Gruenerwald opened the Canyon Colorado Equid Sanctuary in 1978. The sanctuary is located in northern New Mexico.

Canyon Colorado is home to several species of

endangered equids. Gruenerwald's favorites are a small herd of Grévy's zebras. Safe and well fed, the animals adjust quickly to the 6,000 acres (2,428 hectares) of rocky hills and dusty grassland. The climate is much like their native Africa.

Gruenerwald has paid most of the cost out of his own pocket. One zebra can cost as much as $20,000! If he can save the species, this oilman-turned-conservationist thinks the money will have been well spent.

Gruenerwald and naturalists around the world continue to study the zebra and its lifestyle. The more they learn, the more they'll be able to help the zebras survive in their changing world. Compromises between African farmers and the zebra herds will be supervised by naturalists so that both groups can use the land. Zoos will continue to breed healthy zebras so that the animal will never be in danger of extinction.

And the old argument will continue among naturalists — what *is* the real color of this animal — black or white?

MAP:

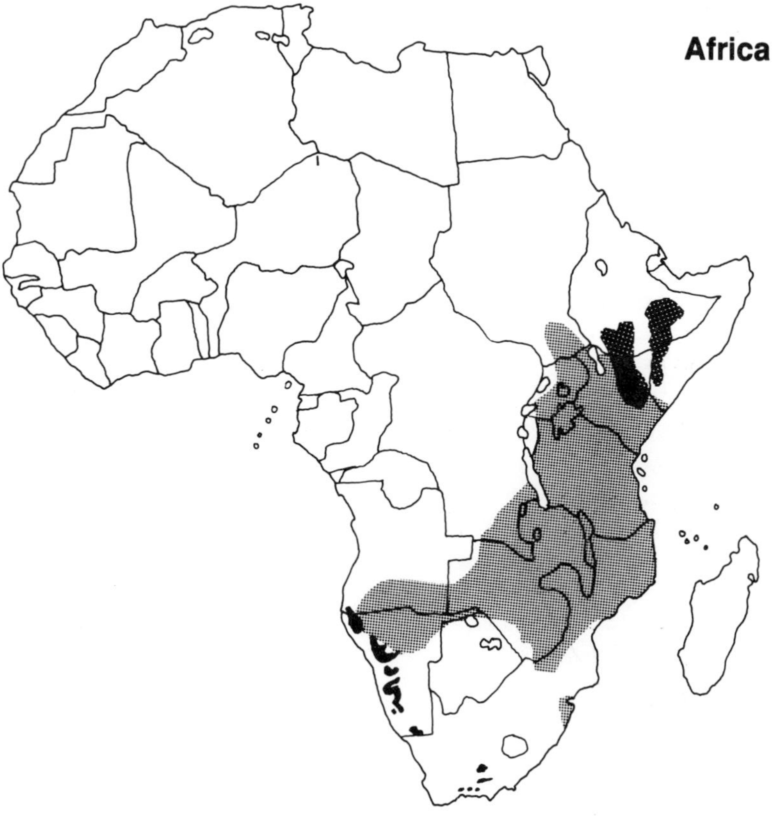

Most Grévy zebras live within these areas.

Most mountain zebras live within these areas.

Most plains zebras live within these areas.

INDEX/GLOSSARY:

46

INDEX/GLOSSARY:

WILDLIFE
HABITS & HABITAT

READ AND ENJOY THE SERIES:

If you would like to know more about all kinds of wildlife, you should take a look at the other books in this series.

You'll find books on bald eagles and other birds. Books on alligators and other reptiles. There are books about deer and other big-game animals. And there are books about sharks and other creatures that live in the ocean.

In all of the books you will learn that life in the wild is not easy. But you will also learn what people can do to help wildlife survive. So read on!